A Note to Parents

Eyewitness Readers is a compelling new program for beginning readers, designed in conjunction with leading literacy experts, including Dr. Linda Gambrell, President of the National Reading Conference and past board member of the International Reading Association.

Eyewitness has become the most trusted name in illustrated books, and this new series combines the highly visual *Eyewitness* approach with engaging, easy-to-read stories. Each *Eyewitness Reader* is guaranteed to capture a child's interest while developing his or her reading skills, general knowledge, and love of reading.

The four levels of *Eyewitness Readers* are aimed at different reading abilities, enabling you to choose the books that are exactly right for your children:

Level 1, for **Preschool to Grade 1**
Level 2, for **Grades 1 to 3**
Level 3, for **Grades 2 and 3**
Level 4, for **Grades 2 to 4**

The "normal" age at which a child begins to read can be anywhere from three to eight years old, so these levels are intended only as a general guideline.

No matter which level you select, you can be sure that you are helping your child learn to read, then read to learn!

A DK PUBLISHING BOOK

Project Editors Mary Atkinson
and Carey Combe
Art Editor Karen Lieberman
Senior Editor Linda Esposito
Production Josie Alabaster
Photography Ray Moller

Reading Consultant
Linda B. Gambrell, Ph.D.

First American Edition, 1998
2 4 6 8 10 9 7 5 3 1
Published in the United States by
DK Publishing, Inc.
95 Madison Avenue, New York, New York 10016

Visit us on the World Wide Web at http://www.dk.com

Copyright © 1998 Dorling Kindersley Limited, London

Published in Great Britain by Dorling Kindersley Limited.

Library of Congress Cataloging-in-Publication Data
Surprise puppy / by Judith Walker-Hodge. -- 1st American ed.
p.   cm. -- (Eyewitness readers. Level 1)
Summary: Describes what is involved when a puppy comes to stay
with a family.
ISBN 0-7894-3624-8 (pbk.)
ISBN 0-7894-3765-1 (hardcover : alk. paper)
1. Puppies--Juvenile literature. [1. Dogs 2. Pets.]
I. Title. II. Series.
SF426.5.H585   1998
636.7'07--dc21   98-20851
                                                CIP
                                                AC

Color reproduction by Colourscan, Singapore
Printed and bound in Belgium by Proost

The publisher would like to thank the following:
Animal Ark for supplying the puppy;
Demi Gray, Jack Gray, Francesca Agati,
and Christopher Gunning for modeling.

The publisher would like to thank the following for
their kind permission to reproduce the photographs:
Eye Ubiquitous: 27 t; Robert Harding: 27 b.

EYEWITNESS READERS

Level 1
PRESCHOOL-GRADE

Surprise Puppy!

Written by Judith Walker-Hodge

DK PUBLISHING, INC.

On Friday afternoon,
Dad brought home
a surprise.

"Look what I've got," he said.
"It's a puppy!
He belongs to
a friend of mine.

"Will you look after him
for a few days?"

"Yes! Yes!"
shouted the twins.

puppy

"The puppy's wagging his tail," said Sam.

"That means he likes us," said Jessica.

"My friend wants
you to name him,"
Dad told the twins.

"I want to call him Wags,"
said Jessica.

"Wags is a good name,"
said Sam.

Wags ran around the room.

"He wants to play," said Dad.
"He needs lots of exercise."

Sam looked in the box of things
that had come with Wags.
He found a toy ball.

He threw the ball
into the garden.
"Fetch," he called.

Wags chased the ball.
But ...

... he did not bring
the ball back.

He just sat
by the ball
and wagged
his tail!

"Wags doesn't know
how to fetch," said Jessica.

"Let's teach him this weekend,"
said Sam.

"Good idea," said Dad.
"Then next week
you can show your friends
what he can do."

Later that evening,
Dad couldn't find
his slippers.

"Oh no!" cried Jessica.
"Wags has your slippers.
He's chewing them!"

"He's teething,"
Dad told her.

"Give him a dog chew.
There's one in the box
with Wags's things."

chew

Soon it was bedtime.
"Can Wags sleep with me?"
Sam asked.

"Wags is too young," said Dad.
"He has to sleep in the kitchen.

"Put some newspaper
on the floor
in case he needs to pee.

"Fill up
his water bowl.

"Then lay a blanket
in his basket
to keep him warm."

basket

On Saturday morning,
the twins rushed
into the kitchen.

Wags jumped up at them.
He was happy
to see them.

"Get down, Wags,"
said Mom.
"Puppies must learn
not to jump up
at people."

"Do puppies eat cornflakes?"
asked Sam.

"Don't be silly.
Puppies eat puppy food,"
said Jessica.
"Mom is feeding Wags now."

Mom filled Wags's
food bowl
with puppy food.

Then she filled
Wags's water bowl
with fresh water.

bowl

That afternoon,
they went to the vet.
Wags needed a checkup.

"Why does Wags need to be
checked by you?" asked Sam.

"To make sure
he is healthy,"
said the vet.

vet

The vet checked Wags carefully.

"Wags has a shiny coat
and a wet nose.
That means
he's well,"
she said.

On Sunday,
the family took Wags
for a long walk.
They went to the park.

Sam and Jessica took turns holding the leash.

"I wish we had a puppy," said Jessica.

"Puppies are hard work," Dad told her.

"We don't mind!" shouted the twins.

leash

After the walk,
everyone went inside.

Jessica hung Wags's leash
on the coat rack.

Sam put
fresh water
in Wags's
water bowl.

No one noticed that
the gate was open.

No one ...
except Wags!

"Where's Wags?"
Dad asked
a few minutes later.

"Oh no,
the gate's open!"
cried Jessica.
"Wags ran away."

"Come on,
let's find him,"
said Mom.

But he wasn't on the street.

And he wasn't in the park.

"I found him!" called Jessica.
Wags was next door.
He had been rolling
in some mud.

Mom brought him home
and gave him a bath.

"We have to keep
the gate shut,"
she told
the twins.

"Okay," said Jessica
as she dried Wags with a towel.

"Sorry," said Sam.
He brushed Wags's coat
with the dog brush.

towel

On Monday,
it was the
twins' birthday.

Mom gave them a tiny box
and Jessica opened it.

"It's a tag!" she said.
"It has our address on it ...
and it says WAGS!"

"It's a dog tag,"
said Dad.
"Wags belongs
to you two now.
This weekend was a test.
You passed with flying colors!"

dog tag

WAGS

Picture Word List

puppy

page 5

vet

page 21

chew

page 13

leash

page 23

basket

page 15

towel

page 29

bowl

page 19

dog tag

WAGS
page 31